BOA
EDITIONS LTD

EVERY
HARD
SWEETNESS

EVERY
HARD
SWEETNESS

Poems by
Sheila Carter-Jones

AMERICAN POETS CONTINUUM SERIES, NO. 205
BOA EDITIONS, LTD. ~ ROCHESTER, NY ~ 2024

First Edition
23 24 25 26 7 6 5 4 3 2 1

For information about permission to reuse any material from this book, please contact The Permissions
Company at www.permissionscompany.com or e-mail permdude@gmail.com.

Publications by BOA Editions, Ltd.—a not-for-profit corporation under section 501 (c) (3) of the United
States Internal Revenue Code—are made possible with funds from a variety of sources, including public
funds from the Literature Program of the National Endowment for the Arts; the New York State Council
on the Arts, a state agency; and the County of Monroe, NY. Private funding sources include the Max
and Marian Farash Charitable Foundation; the Mary S. Mulligan Charitable Trust; the Rochester
Area Community Foundation; the Ames-Amzalak Memorial Trust in memory of Henry Ames, Semon
Amzalak, and Dan Amzalak; the LGBT Fund of Greater Rochester; and contributions from many
individuals nationwide. See Colophon on page 137 for special individual acknowledgments.

Cover Art and Design: Sandy Knight
Interior Design and Composition: Isabella Madeira
BOA Logo: Mirko

BOA Editions books are available electronically through BookShare, an online distributor offering
Large-Print, Braille, Multimedia Audio Book, and Dyslexic formats, as well as through e-readers that
feature text to speech capabilities.

Cataloging-in-Publication Data is available from the Library of Congress.

BOA Editions, Ltd.
250 North Goodman Street, Suite 306
Rochester, NY 14607
www.boaeditions.org
A. Poulin, Jr., Founder (1938–1996)

PRAISE FOR *EVERY HARD SWEETNESS*

"What happens to the body and soul when your 'blood' is brutalized? In *Every Hard Sweetness* Sheila Carter-Jones witnesses the 'goneness' of the body as her father is enslaved and taken to the State Hospital for the Criminal Insane for the crime of being black. With stunning imagery and astonishing voice, she recovers memory, rescripts it, takes us through doors of unbearable cruelty: *I make my body a wall.*

There is a gate to goneness that only Sheila Carter-Jones knows, the gate her father passed through, and with original form and movement she speaks it—the *hard sweetness* of survival, the animal nature of the state as it hunts a man because of his dark skin, the heartbreak of prices paid—years of courage and anger to 'realign the stars.' This book is unforgettable in its bravery, its truth-telling, its tragedy, its strength."

—Jan Beatty, author of *The Body Wars*

"*Every Hard Sweetness* is an extraordinary work of history and possibility. Within the brutal conditions of every state-sanctioned terror against her family, the poet makes a brilliant record of a deeply disciplined, steadfast tenderness. Placing her art practice beside that of her father's, she asks readers to think with her about personal, familial, and national imaginations. Out of these conditions, Sheila Carter-Jones creates a stunning, experimental work that pushes on the edges of what language can even hold, making a work that asks its readers to engage in an ongoing practice of attention, scrutiny, and care. These arrangements touch me into new thinking and feeling, across time."

—Aracelis Girmay, author of *the black maria*

"In *Every Hard Sweetness*, Sheila Carter-Jones refracts a personal story and larger history of America: her father's unjust six-and-half-year incarceration in a mental hospital in the 1960s and her coming-of-age and coming to terms with the trauma of her family's story is set against the backdrop of the Civil Rights Movement and the ongoing struggle for freedom for Black Americans. Carter-Jones powerfully wields various forms, including photographs, to recover the past, resulting in a work that is a moving testament to the "art of staying alive." In poem after poem, Carter-Jones counters erasure, fearlessly "filling the geography of silence."

—Shara McCallum, author of *No Ruined Stone*

"Sheila Carter-Jones' *Every Hard Sweetness* is a remarkable chronicle of survivorship and resistance with respect to Civil Rights' era atrocities and their legacies. This astonishing book breaks silence about the 'gone-dead'—a practice in which Black men labeled as 'troublemakers' were arrested and forcibly removed from their homes and families, then wrongfully incarcerated in institutions for the criminally insane. Carter-Jones' father was one of the 'gone-dead' who disappeared into 'cold storage' for over seven years for speaking up and speaking out. In powerful and incandescent poems, Carter-Jones deftly navigates the ongoing repercussions of this haunting family history—revealing cultural contexts of colorism, misogynoir, and white supremacy. This extraordinary and important book illustrates the ways in which anti-Black violence can be brutally whitewashed under the guise of institutional and bureaucratic complicity. At the same time, *Every Hard Sweetness* insists on celebrating Black courage, Black resilience, and Black joy in poems that are riveting, heartbreaking, and gorgeous."

—Lee Ann Roripaugh, author of *Tsunami vs. the Fukushima 50*

For my mother and father, with gratitude

I shall become, I shall become a collector of me. And put meat on my soul.
—Sonia Sanchez

CONTENTS

1.

PROLOGUE

There is no margin on these pages of skin history. We locals know each other. What we do and why. How we say what we mean. How we live together huddled in small spaces between words where dirt roads intersect and curve back to a past not distant from the present. We know who we are in the equation of a certain period of time. Time when a rabbit's foot, a wishbone, a juju mask, a four-leaf clover, a blue bird, or a falling star will not bring good luck. Time when we know we need a body of courage. We know it is not a messiah. We know it is an Everyday woman; an ordinary man.

DEAR _____,

This letter   context   First   I hope in reading   you   experience   in a way
never been felt or known up to now   poems tell   people   trauma There is also
trees, flowers and other objects

I'm the girl   sometimes I am   I feel   The life of each   though   can be   may well
be the   someone you know   even you   bend   toward it as if opening in
sunlight Meet it in its epicenter   see what you   Feel what you   engage

1960's   black body   fought back   resistance based on joy
taking action   creating a realm in which one belongs to oneself   sites for such
joy against my father's   my mother's   and my   However this joy against
site of many bodies   yours

The   interconnectedness of   in our fluids In   words   Images
and meandering of blood-rhythms   motion chipping away   centuries
silence shame weakness downright hurt   release ache and fear   strengthen joy of
belonging to self

Before   and before   burdened with   violence of silence I   a happy child
in happy family   happy community We belonged   I remember joy   history
 Fact 1 August 6 1965   Voting Rights Act   law   Fact 2 June that same
father   hunted   captured   in road-trap   two hired detectives two small
town cops   Had he seen   heard   doing yardwork for   rich white
Shortly   a mock hearing   his body stolen   far from home   away   to
State Hospital for the Criminally Insane.

Put away Put away Put away Put mountains away from home   Second life they say
in rolling wooded countryside   north of Poconos   Up North   North   Green
trees bend   Bending   Hush   Hush sweet darlin'   Rough beast slouching
to be born

In Starlight

GONE-DEAD

(adj.) describes
a person, mostly a man,
mostly a black or brown
man forcibly incarcerated,
not insane not convicted
of a crime, considered a
troublemaker; sometimes
a man held due to
bureaucratic error

(n.) place
where one is forcibly held
against his will, geographic
location between the seen
and the unseen, space between
the living and the dead, body
as a site of brutal, inhumane
treatment, use of mood altering
drugs, a place where one can
easily be forgotten to
have ever existed

See also
goneness, slave ship, holding-pen,
auction block, plantation, lynch,
patty-roller, jail, prison, chain gang,
labor-camp, concentration camp,
internment camp, extermination
camp, detained, state hospital,
history

Only picture of my father as a child. Maybe four years old.

DARK BOY

It is a story about my father. My mother
whispered it even when he wasn't around
and couldn't hear. The first time I heard
the story, it scared me. It began with his
mother, Ruth, who was ashamed of my
father's skin. It was too dark for her to
love. Until then, I didn't know love apart
from skin. It is how I began to notice
difference. Unlike Ruth's first boy born
red-brown and the girl born with cornmeal
yellow skin, my father's complexion was
a curse cast on Ruth's belly. He was born
dark and illegitimate. Evil from the start is
how people judged him by his color. He
was mistake enough, yet became the stain
that his mother made and because of his
darkness, he was labeled troublemaker
by sight.

DAY OF THE DEAD VOICE - LE MONSIEUR NOIR

Every act of creation is first of all an act of destruction.
—Pablo Picasso

An artist stole beauty from flesh of wood. Painted angular planes and bold shapes like patterns of scarification carved by Jim Crow Laws.

Labeled Troublemaker is a type of scarification. The technique requires stripping skin from the voice and rearranging pieces of tongue.

When two local cops in uniform came hunting for my father, one wore a trinket of hammered silver. A tarnished image hanging on a cross.

Fists worked as sharp instruments to reshape his face into an American mask. Marking the body was holy.

Shards of emotional intensity were punched in to create a face of geometric distortion. A trademark of disfigured joy.

Despite the fractured appearance, what was left was a reddish-brown imprint of the real. An abstract of the face.

To enhance the exhibition of features no mouth was carved in. The mask was made without possibility for speech, so it could not talk back.

Other American mask-makers and newspapers, too, were abuzz with wild stories of safaris, umbrella trees, exotic animals, and Civil Rights.

No article included names of the policemen who caught my father in a road trap and called him a son-of-a-bitch gone ape.

No mention of the mouth that bit into his bicep, left teeth marks that branded and showed a pattern of lineage.

The mask was praised as a signature piece. It's features became law—instructive. How beauty is mandated.

SHE COULDN'T DO ANYTHING BUT GET LOST

My mother got lost on her way home
from the county jail.

She said my father asked
her a thousand times if
she wanted to move to
the city and she said, No
a thousand times.

She had no need to go downtown for
any reason. So, she didn't.

The A&P was minutes
away by car and the garden
was lined with rows of
corn, tomatoes, red peppers,
and string beans climbed on
vines as collards unfurled
their green.

That summer the city was burning.
She didn't sweat. Until now. There was
a mock hearing last minute quick
before lunch-time.

My father was brought in.
Cuffed. Judged by no jury.
Rich men in seersucker,
pinstripe-straight said, Frank
is a madman. His voice is
insane. Put that nigger away
until he learns to not
talk back.

My mother said she couldn't find
the right bus-stop. Her head was
reeling in twists and turns. She made it
home sometime after ten o'clock.

A GODDESS COMES DOWN TO EARTH

This hill is mine.
I climbed it to prove
I am brave as any boy. No technique.
No style, just grab and hold.

Now, Goddess on earth
I sit in the hazelnut grove
crack shells with a trophy rock.
Eat the fruit.

A bucktooth boy I tease finds me here.
His breath a spray of
spit and words say,
They got your dad.

I know who They are and run. I don't
hear fists and kicks.
Not blood, not cuffs, or
my sandals on gravel.

My head flies up
past trees with long thin
seed pods hanging motionless as a bird
shot on the wing.

I land at home. Bang
on the locked door.
Little Randy's eyes are already rubbed
empty of a man
gone-dead.

How do I say I am afraid to cross over?
Enter a ghastly silence
that allures like
a phantom heart
aching to exist.

Can I dare be brave as any boy who feels
the absence of a father?

FISSURED

How do I say
I am afraid to cross the threshold,
enter the body of a house where they
came to disappear a man. Should I
willingly become an innocent bride to
darkness—let it lift and carry me over
—keep secret its doings in the long
twilight of a man gone-dead?

They came for him.
The man who has ability to create his
own image. They came for him. To
steal his too big voice that gathers.
Demands. Dares disrupt like a crack in
the kitchen wall making its own path as
it opens to bear obvious weight of
things that have become normal and
settled over time.

I make my body a wall.
To not cause the crack to deepen, widen,
and grow longer. I plaster a smile. Tape
myself shut so no words destroy my silent
aesthetic. Insert a peep-hole between two
realities. With tiny gestures I put fork to
mouth. I eat but do not taste sweet, sour
or salty. Only bitter.

HARD SWEETNESS

My mother said, In front of your face they
laugh and talk with you. But, when you turn
your back, you're still nothin' but a nigger to 'em.
And don't you ever forget it.

I felt her strength push into me so hard I didn't
dare fold or turn to look elsewhere. Not under
that stone-eyed ache she sang into me like
the song she hummed when wringing clothes with
her hands. And don't get twisted up, she said.

Her face flushed to full magenta. Her earthiness,
beautiful. Beautiful black woman. Holding
her whole body shouldered against the rush.

ARCHITECTURE OF BETWEENNESS

Victorian-style. Drenched-red brick,
granite firm in its hardness. Could be
a monastery with its secluded vows or
a military school with its rock hard
training. But, is neither. It is a socially
constructed structure between existence
and non-existence. Windows with glass
eyes serve their ornamental purpose of
blindness in sight. Like my father's
upper front tooth that fell out years later
at the dinner table, but there was no
blood left to give. It was replaced with
a false one. He said it was for cosmetics.

I IMAGINE MY FATHER AT THE GATE TO THE STATE HOSPITAL FOR THE CRIMINALLY INSANE

He stands. A man. Forced. Handcuffed.
A ray of sun glints against gentle brown
skin. The light makes his red rimmed
eyes flutter like two petals of a rose that
shiver in a storm. He looks up at bars
until the back of the skull rests on top of
the spine. The cervical vertebrae that
allows him to nod, Yes, sir. No, sir.

Bars go high up like the bean-stalk Jack
climbed to a make believe land in
the sky. Unless the black bars turn into
magic beans, there is no geography of
imagination beyond them. No fairy-tale
made real except for the smell of blood.
The sound of bones being cracked.

Ordinary men, like giant ogres will keep
the man gone-dead, hidden in sprawling
beauty of Pennsylvania Mountains. They
protect years of stone-hard infrastructure.
And, as any family man would, they
work to take care of their own castles—
wives and children they love. And they
are violent, too.

Inside the gate they redistribute weight of
duty. Their at home bodies swell with
growl and bark, cryptic as any God who
breeds fear. Monster feet in steel-toe boots
demand to keep the head turned. Away
from truth. Keep the body tense, braced
for the next kick.

When they finish terrorizing their captives,
all creep home. Transform—become
normal as any man who wants his children
to have more than he ever had. They say,
That's how it is. I did my job.

THE PRODIGIOUS POUCH

Her fingers rip paper as if to get at silences that have been stored in a throat pouch until she almost says words out loud.

Her hands shake so badly she takes a butter knife from the kitchen drawer and slices across the top edge of an envelope.

The wife and daughter have heard nothing for three months when this letter comes flying out of the blue that is not like a sky.

The girl sees the swooping beak of the cursive letter *F.* It is how the man begins his name. Wide mouthed like a pelican.

The open pouch *F* is the way the man begins to hold his family, until they can hold themselves together.

The wife and daughter have been waiting in the dark for news. The letter is a bit hazy and does not shine bright enough for clarity.

There is no date. It begins Dear M. Somewhere just past the middle is a question that asks about the daughter. Then kiss-kiss, kiss-kiss. Love, *F.*

The girl knows he asked about her because the mother read that part aloud. She kept the other words between herself and the paper.

Or, between herself and the space of a man gone-dead. This is the first letter that has arrived at the post office, box 110.

It could have been the fourth or fifth, or the tenth or twelfth letter the husband handed to guards to mail for him.

One thing for sure. If there was no money involved, the letter sure wasn't going anywhere, except to the trash can.

How did the man get money after three months of no communication with home? Or, was there no money involved? Or, necessary?

Was it a test to see if the woman and the girl would stay silent to keep officials and guards from being nervous? Or, a test to keep the man alive?

As if there is power in silence the mother and daughter scoop letters from words and squeeze the secret arrangement of meaning into their pouches.

The woman and girl tighten their jaw muscles as if to purge the desire to speak or to question. They hold their heads high. Eyes closed against the plunge.

I IMAGINE THE GATE TO THE STATE HOSPITAL FOR THE CRIMINALLY INSANE

Riding for five hours I imagine the gate at the entrance to
the state hospital for the gone-dead. It is like the one that
swings open on Oak Drive where rich kids I go to school
with live. Each black bar is tipped with a metal shaped
arrowhead, razor sharp to cut straight through to soft tissue.
There's no escaping wealth. It's in the muscle and fat of
the institution. The gate's hinges for the unhinged keep
what's wanted in. What's not, out. Bars like ribs surround
the heart of the establishment. Protect it by law. When we
get close, I see the gate is wide open. We pass through a
bent chain-link fence that's chest high on a six-foot man. I
imagine I can hurl myself over with a running start. My
father could hurdle it. Walk home. There have been higher
leaps and longer distances to begin again. As the car drifts
toward a tiny building, I expect to see a man in uniform. If
he waves us in, I know his welcome will be condescending.
His words hard as flint. If a gun is holstered on his hip, a
nickel-plated handle will protrude to dare a wrong move.
Or, word. Or, tone of voice. I keep the gate that separates
me from school snobs in my head to ground myself in what
I know. How far I have come. Yet, still question how much
farther to see my father between now and home. No guard
stops us. Questions us. We park between tire-worn yellow
lines. Boundaries marked for visitors. The place is quiet.
Not peacefully quiet, but hauntingly still. And, the bucolic
landscape fills me with the geography of silence.

HARD SWEETNESS

Do not, my mother said, read
the world only through eyes of
the heart. Do not be kind without
thinking eyes, my mother said,
to save me from going blind.

STARS OVER CINCINNATI

After the Greyhound Bus breaks city lines, it hits the open highway like a rabid dog. Everything is vaster than all the small-town backyards, the tallest oak carved with fresh cut hearts of love and there are scars too. I slump in the seat. Feel some release as if stones I've carried from the creek are falling out of me. Their denseness gives way to rush of darkness and pretending to be untouched by troubled people in our house and I am one of them.

Faking made it easy to convince my mother that I am old enough to take the bus by myself. When the driver smiles at me in the rear-view mirror, I smile back. I still have some trust for men in uniform, but if he smiles too long, I look away. I've seen hardness behind a man's smile like his.

The window reflects a mass of dark-girl that blends with a pool of sleep. I dream that dream. Always a man coming through the back door. His black boots rustle old newspaper that covers freshly mopped linoleum. I run and run. He chases. I never see his face. Only the black boots as I run in darkness.

When the bus brakes, it jolts my body awake. I am breathless. My heart thumps. The bus shakes and makes guttural sounds like an old dog sleeping and farting in some wild animal dream. It's the first rest-stop in Ohio.

The driver grabs the rail, swings down, stands outside the door like a good soldier. I get off to stretch. He asks if I want to go to the terminal's roof. Look at the stars over Cincinnati. I know these flecks of light are no different than what I see from my backyard. And, I had assured my mother.

Back on the bus I remember learning patterns in the dark. How each star's light faded on a trail my fourth grade eyes traced, until I mapped a shape against blackness. The Big Dipper, Cassiopeia, Ursa Major and Minor. Orion the hunter. When the driver gets back on, he drops his mud-green eyes. I chart him in a long line of men in uniform.

2.

HARD SWEETNESS

She said I was pulled from the womb into
the 12:01 dark ticking toward dawn with
eyes questioning the world beyond the amniotic
sac. Said I was born with a caul of embryonic
skin covering my head. My small hands naturally
balled into fists. Said I was born with my daddy
in me. Ready to realign the pattern of stars.

SMALL HANDS

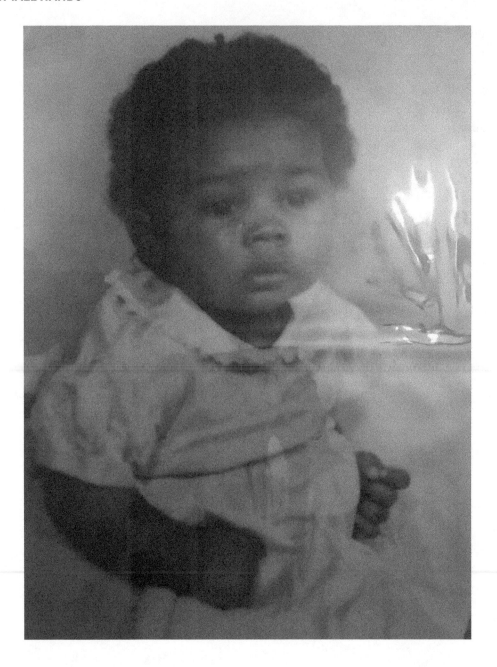

ANATOMY OF A SYSTEM

A jar of formaldehyde at the back of the room
is labeled Bullfrog. Kingdom: Animalia. Phylum:
Chordata. Class: Amphibia. The biology teacher
stands in front leading a review. Holds
up each organ of a frog's dismembered body.
Clasped in tweezers, each part dangles.

I don't know yet how men are classified
at the state hospital for the criminal
insane. I only know that my father is
there. I don't know that men are labeled.
Race: Black/Negro. Gender: Male.
Attitude: Threatening. Mental Capacity:
Twelve-year-old. Notes: seems to have
his own philosophy about his place in
society. Diagnosis: Schizophrenic.

On the day of the test the frog is spread
around the room. Each piece of its innards
stretched on a bed of cotton is held taut
with straight pins to keep it from shriveling.
Clipboard in hand, I walk to each station.
Identify the organ or glob of flesh. A white
boy behind me pokes the hard edge of
his pressed particle board into the small of
my back. He pushes to see my answers.

I don't know yet the answers institution
officials give to questions about the
death of a man. That when his body is
exhumed it is empty. All of the internal
organs gone. Even his brain. Official
cause of death recorded—heart attack.

I record answers on my paper.
The white boy is breathing on my neck.
I hold my clipboard up for him to see.
After he copies liver, I erase it. Write
heart. After he copies stomach, I scratch it.
Write large intestine.

I don't know yet that guards kick a man
in the stomach so hard he shits himself.
His abdomen cramps for five years. For
three months he pisses blood.

When the bell rings I erase testes.
Write brain.

I don't know yet that my father will be
systematically erased for six and a half
years. That he will rewrite his life as
he reorients his body to—not pinned
down.

FACTS

I slink into a hole of darkness
as in a fairytale and vanish under

the 7th grade desk. My tongue
presses against embarrassment.

Teeth clench hard to hold silence
steady in my mouth when

the teacher teaches that slaves loved
to sing for their masters.

He says slaves loved to dance for
their masters. Pictures

in my U.S. history book prove it.

I hold my breath until the teacher
catches me playing deaf and lifts

the desk off the floor with me in
it. Drops me. He insists

I believe these facts and there is
no such thing as falling free.

KITCHEN TEACHER

I learn in the kitchen between corn meal and
week-old Crisco cooking oil. Between pinto
beans and slight meat of neckbones. I ask my
mother questions. Fact check the history teacher.

What's a turbaned mistress of a Blue Grass
kitchen? What's a gingham dress? How is a
woman broad, portly, and stout of heart all
at once?

I want to know what corndodgers are and how
I can make them with government wieners.
I'm really asking what makes a man a troublemaker?
What gets him all rolled up in the wrong way and
makes him distasteful? And, what should I say
when a teacher asks for my father's name—
for the records?

She says, Say his name. He's still your dad. Don't
add anything for flavor. She's teaching me
the careful practice of unsounding the silence of
a man gone-dead.

She says, Don't get wrapped up in made-up facts.
I follow her directions:

Roll the wieners in soft dough.

Have a griddle hot. Careful not

to burn my hands. Bake

the corndodgers thoroughly until

a rich brown. Not like the fact of

Jesse Washington's body burnt

to a crisp. May 15, 1916.

Waco, Texas.

HIS BODY HOLDS SILENCE

—a conversation between a patient and his mother; and between the mother and a man called doctor at the state hospital

Named after Robert Jackson
and nicknamed Stonewall, too,
his voice slams silence against
the old pattern
          to break
          a man.

He
tells his Mother, They
(guards of the institution)
          are going
          to k-k-kill
          me.
I don't have long
          Zong to live.

The Mother
inquires of a man called doctor
(who is not a doctor)
          Why
          are you mistr-
          eating
          my son?

A man called doctor
(who is not a doctor)
replies,

> Your son
> won't
> talk.
> Stub-
> born.
> We
> are going
> to break
> his sin,
> cinder-
> block head.

PRISONERS ROUND

—The state hospital for the criminally insane is a psychiatric hospital referred to as the Animal Farm. It is without a board-certified psychiatrist and has no job training. They don't figure on many leaving.

A series of movements. Repeated tasks. Create.
Recreate oneself step by step. Walk single file.
Walk in a circle. In the same direction. Walk.
Walk in a shuffling cadence. One behind
the other. Walk to stay alive. Walk a thin line
between human and trapped animal.

       This is training.

If not walking, workshop areas mold a man into
a desired form—the guards' hobby. Favored
men rotate in. They know rules—Do not
scuff the floors. Turn your eyes away. Search
the ceiling for angels. Mop up the blood.

       This is training.

Keep feet, eyes, hands, doing something to
keep from being held down by a boot. Make
ashtrays, weave wallets from empty cigarette
packs, caste small Christmas trees for guards
to take outside and sell or give as cheap gifts.
They make paintings of John F. Kennedy and
Jesus. Everyone's favorite saviors.

       This is training to save oneself.

CIGARETTE CURRENCY

CAMEL-CHESTERFIELD-KOOL-PALL MALL-WINSTON
Blended. Slow burning. Taste so good. Most refreshing wherever
particular people congregate.

Designed to show how a man was forced
to live. He sent three handmade woven-paper
wallets home. One survived. Holds no dollar
bills. Only memories of how he and his family
got by tucked between tightly folded creases.

STRINGING

There has always been a medium-sized pine
to decorate. Every year, the same frosty
colored ornaments to hang from branches.
Recycled silver tinsel to drape over needles
as if to cover their flair for natural sharpness.
Red garland is always shorter at the end of
each season until what is left hangs from
two or three branches like pieces of old ideas
losing their effect. What hangs on, I save in
a box marked X-mas. Next year, I will pop
popcorn. String kernels together with a needle
and thread from the tin sewing box to make
a homemade decoration. It will be the end of
1965. The year I read Malcolm X is eulogized
as our shining black Savior; who didn't
hesitate to die because he loved us so. That
his friends took up the gravediggers' shovels
that February to complete the burial. June
that same year a man is taken. Gone
dead-insane for protesting. Entombed in an
asylum. August, the right to vote is signed into
law. Not the Savior's and not the gone-dead
man's voices are counted. Come December, I
hang the same frosty colored balls. Place shreds
of tinsel dull as sterling dinnerware my mother
polishes for a rich woman she cleans for.
The plastic star I place on top is scratched and
fragile—about to crack.

TREE IN A BOX

It is in a box
covered with brown
grocery bag paper.

I can tell my father
wrapped it with his
unbelievably weathered

hands coated with
the patina of other
men's greed and belief.

The paper is cut straight
along pressed folds and
is neatly taped.

Corners snapped
in hard creases stand
at attention with the same

stiffness as starched
pants of the chauffeur's
uniform he wore while

driving a rich lady who
was always right with her
legendary Bloody Mary in

hand and money enough to
pay for his smile that masked
silent humiliation.

I untie the twine strung twice
around the box and knotted
with no need for a pretty bow.

The Wayne County Herald
balled and strategically stuffed
inside the box holds

its contents from being jostled
about. I reach in and feel
the tip of a fragile hardness.

Careful as pulling a stillborn
from a gleam in the eye
I lift the tree out and every-

thing changes for the child.
Fifteen-by-twelve inches of
clay—molded, baked and glazed

means a man is still alive
because he practiced shaping a
life of worth—outwitting those

with money enough to buy a
man like him.

STRING TALK

I say the hole in the tree trunk is seeking blackness.
He says he sees through from another time.

I say the emptiness is longing for substance.
He says no such thing as completely seen.

I say breath is everything.
He says expanding space is genetic.

I say what about the fruits hanging.
He says he sees them always from beyond the veil.

I say I am looking for a cornucopia.
He says no utopia exists apart from string theory.

I say the first yank must snap the stem.
He says the first bite crackles skin.

I say I climbed an apple tree.
He asks if some branches vibrated.

I say I have to ask my mother about that.
He says everything is stored in the tissues.

I say the fruits were shriveled face-knots.
He asks if I tasted the bitter pulp.

I say my lips scrunched up in loops of braided roots.
He says he's in the dimension of dormant buds.

I say everything comes to pass by way of kinfolk.
He says no girl in her right mind talks to trees.

I say I have never been in my right mind.
He says an ideal black body has a characteristic frequency.

I say I hear hush.
He says I'm swinging.

TREE WITH A MOUTH

Could the old ones be passing information through root grafts?—unions where roots of different trees splice into a single voice like veins grow together in a healing skin graft. This is how to travel underground. Plod against the stone. Live beyond the veil. Many dark bodies teaching oneness. My father's consciousness among them encodes rhythms in me.

THE FLOWERING

—And there are buds that cannot bloom at all/ In the light, but crumple, piteous, and
fall;/ So in the dark we hide the heart that bleeds,

—Countee Cullen

Men gather for the five-on-one tactic to
turn another man into an object to be
thrown. Ten hands grab a piece of body.
Swing the man by ankle, by wrist, and by
fistfuls of flesh. Throw him flying like a
ball flung from left-field where the un-
breakable are broken for fun. They watch
the man wave his arms for balance, fix his
legs and curl into himself. A split moment
of clarity is all the body needs to remember
how life began to take shape. He thinks he
smells bacon. Sees his mother shuffling her
body across the kitchen. Hears her voice
warn to pull his head from beneath blankets
and get ready for school. He hears the knob
jiggle and sees her on the porch waiting for
a car to take her to a house where she will
tend little white children. She vanishes
the instant his body hits the concrete floor.
He does not bounce back. He opens.

ENTRANCE DOWN

At the end of a long corridor
                          is

              a door

                  to take

                      a body

                          down.

EULOGY FOR THE UNCLAIMED

—In the basement morgue of the State Hospital for the criminally insane, a patient calls out praise for the dead. His other personality responds.

For six and one-half years a dark man is sentenced to be a gone-dead body here at the state hospital for the criminally insane. Is he a criminal?
No.
Is he insane?
No.
Is he gone?
Yes.
He is an example of a man standing up. Hidden for now. If he is a lucky one he will leave here alive. Not like the weight I have slumped over my shoulder. Is this one dead?
Yes.
I have carried him down from the infirmary unit into this hole of little light and heaved his battered body onto the butcher's table. Do we need to know his name?
No.
He shall be nameless as all others who have been brought down by dark habits. Look around this room lit by undiscerning light. See here, jars lining shelves? See organs drowning in them? One lung is blackened and charred from emphysema. See there, a brain in a display container. See how the thin tissue wraps around itself. Holds on to short and long term memories?
Yes.

I say k-plop. Here is another cadaver I drop to the underbelly of medical science. Or, to the black-market. Fresh meat for the butcher's rib cutter. To splay the body.
Get to the interior.
Remove all questions he dared ask,
all promises made,
his allergic reaction to fresh peaches.
Separate out the way he threw his head back and dropped
grapes into his mouth one at a time.
Sever connective tissues without tenderness with which he stroked his wife's hair.
Pull from the bone words he said nobody wanted to hear.
After all this, and this isn't all…
When the heart is lifted from the cavity, it will be firm and show no signs of having failed. It will remain unrestrained, courageous, and full of irrepressible love.

GONE DEAD

Good men are gone-dead before the rising sun
begins its fierce ascent upward to burning noon;
shine light, shine black on inhumane deeds done.

One sweep of light counts good men as none
and none will be peaceful in black sod of gloom;
good men are gone-dead before the rising sun.

Men hidden away dared speak of bodies flung
to the pattyroller and rolled voiceless to the tomb;
shine light, shine black on inhumane deeds done.

Flesh is trivial until the death wagon has begun
its slow creep beneath a black pinch of moon;
good men are gone-dead before the rising sun.

Diggers in the dark are what watchmen become
with cruelties sized by boot on the shovel of doom;
shine light, shine black on inhumane deeds done.

Silences buried shallow is black dirt on everyone.
Skeletons tell truths when black bones are exhumed.
Good men are gone-dead-black before the rising sun.
Shine light, shine black on inhumane deeds done.

BÊTE NOIR

Who is the black beast now
hungry for the flesh? Who
is a monster and who is not an angel?
In the same domain level is level
frontwards and backwards.
Let evil live. Live evil.

Did he come out alive? the journalist
asked.
Yes, that's what he said. Yes, that's what
I answered.

I was still trying to put my feet
on the floor, trying to get
my head back in orbit.

I begged a demon—make me an
angel, a real one with an iron staff, cloven
feet, wings not feathery but the spiked kind
that cut small slashes quick enough to
make wounds bleed, slow. Sharp like
what I feel when I'm breathless with
hurt and no amount of face drowned in
breasts can take it away.

The journalist said some didn't make it out.
Said some died in there. It hit me. My
conscience shifted, knowing my father
stumbled out of the dark hole of
the criminal insane asylum on the back of
the reaper that rides the underside of every
breath. That's what the man meant when
he asked did he come out alive.

All I cared about was my father and how
he was going to live under shadows of bête
noir monster-men and how he didn't want
anything to do with their heaven, just wanted
to live in as much good as he could. Face
the black beast in daylight—eye to mouth,
teeth to tongue—man to man.

3.

HARD SWEETNESS

Self is made from scratch, my mother said.

Scratch is boundary line.

Scratch is from nothing.

Scratch is from brutally raw materials.

Scratch is starting point of vision.

MY FIRST BOYFRIEND IS A DARK SILHOUETTE OF MOON

A total eclipse happens when
an ordinary man is abducted and packed away
in a place nicknamed cold storage for the way voices
demanding change are clipped. My mother's mind is stolen too,
but her body is still here. Inside the house we teeter
on a narrow orbit called family.
We are shadows unsolicited by sun.
When neighbors ask how I am getting along I say, Pretty good.
A nice thing to say. Pretend a smile. If I say what is true,
I will be saying out loud how I am hurting in my silence. That I am
lost in a small house of cramped shadows bent into corners,
climbing walls and hovering on ceilings.
Light is too harsh for my opaque body.
And, in that space between intense obscurity and faint visibility
a sweet boy my age said he loved me. When he came to the door one
Saturday night, he brought a gift of
spool heel shoes the deep burgundy-brown color of my father's skin.
The suede was soft and new as the boy's
hand that teased my darkness into his body. It didn't matter if
what he felt was love, or not. I just needed
a body to block the light.

QUEEN OF SOUL SISTER

If my father had been home when I was eighteen,
there is no way I would have been at Bell's Bar
where Chuckie played bass guitar with his eyes half
closed. Me, watching him with mine half open. I
was in love and staggering from the way his fingers
strummed the strings so softly sweat meandered down
his sugar-brown skin. He combed his jet-black hair
back on both sides and pumped up on top. Greased
so slick I saw iridescent sheens of blues and maroons
as the strobe light turned. His eyes, black-ice
dangerous, attracted me. And, he had his own car.
A spit-fire red convertible that reared up and clapped
like thunder applauding our take-off as he pressed
the gas pedal straight to the floor. We sped two
headlights bright, parting the dark down Route 910.
The radio blaring Aretha, My friends keep telling
me that you ain't no good. I sat with my eyes
aglitter. My back against the seat. The balls of my
feet grinding the floormat as if there was no such
thing as gradual, a build-up to a kiss. His left hand
gripped the steering wheel. The right hand arced
out of nowhere and fumbled for mine. He held it on
the stick-shift as he changed the gear. My thin sole
sandals pressed harder. Steadied me as if my body
was Earth braced for a star tumbling. And I ain't
never felt a light bursting like that.

RICH LADY'S CAR

We are sitting on the front porch when she,
the rich lady, pulls up. Her half grin says she

sees up into our nappy heads from her wood
paneled station wagon. Its forest green is

so deep we almost lose sight of our dreams.
There's hardly room in the back seat after

all our mothers get in. Shoulder to shoulder.
Packed skin tight like when slave ships sailed.

All our mothers work nonstop to keep a black
home in order and a white one, too. Everyday

they leave from front doors. Enter through back
doors and we count how many swollen ankles it

takes to get the rich lady to show all of her white
teeth. Perfectly straight uppers and lowers that

click shut like the car door and we wave to our
mothers and watch the deep green expel clouds

of exhaust leaving inexhaustible facts not written
in history books. Trails of plunder clogging up

truths be told. We get nervous when the lady's
car is a hazy outline barely seen through black

tail-pipe smoke until the car disappears from
sight. Yet we stare. We wait. Stand guard until

four o'clock comes and we count each woman
as she gets out of the rich lady's car.

AMERICAN BEAUTY: 101

1.

A certain amount of the feminine narcissism must rest ultimately on real physical attactiveness and such attractiveness is determined by the artificial standard each community selects. In this country the standard is blond, blue-eyed, white-skinned girl with regular features. ██ there is not much

████████████ approximation of the ideal. The girl who is black has no option in the matter ████████████

████████████████ She is, in fact, the antithesis of American beauty. ████████████████████████████████████ in this country she is ugly. However loved and prized she may be by her mother, family, and community, she has no real basis of feminine attractiveness on which to build a sound feminine narcissism.

2.

In an addition, she takes her place within a historical context, in which women like her ████████ have been viewed only as ████████████████

████████████████████████████████████

a source of labor: and she has been valued for the amount of work she can perform.

3.

██

USED SLIPPERS

When the rich lady she cleaned for handed her a tattered pair of slippers, my mother smiled. Said she could get some use out of them. Claimed she loved pink.

Even though they were too big and her feet would never grow into them she danced across linoleum as if in a ballroom far from our small kitchen.

Away from tasks, chipped saucers and cracked cups. From scraping food off my plate onto hers to not waste a bit. I didn't get dreamy-eyed over those slippers.

I wanted to tear the marabou feathers off one-by-one as she danced in them holding a chicken wing, stretched apart and hanging over the palm of her hand.

Like a crispy string of pearls drooping, she plucked slivers of sinewy meat and when she held up a cleaned bone it showed how we straddled the edge of poor.

And, though I did not starve to death, I was filled with light from a forty-watt bulb shining on a solo woman two-stepping between rhythms of contradictions.

She is gone twenty years now and I am locked down under threat of disease—even death. Honestly, I don't want to die—think, if not me, who then, will say how

she taught me to dance alone under a brief light—like a firefly flashing in the dark. My small hand reaching up to catch the glow.

LEAVING A SMALL HOUSE FOR COLLEGE KNOWING WHAT I HAVE ALREADY LEARNED

Here in the bucket seat of my brother's new mustang,
my mother on the porch waving good-bye, I see
smoke from her cigarette float up.
I'm already lightheaded.
Try to catch my breath, make sense of silences that
have sheltered me for three years. I'm pulling away from
nights the black radio station played hits from Motown.
There was always music.
Dance contests in the living room, girls against boys—
the Supremes challenging the Temptations.
I was a fragile Diana Ross.
Skinny girl with a wide-open mouth.
Ronrico rum thinning my voice to a high-strung
vibrato. I wanted to be numb. It didn't matter if later,
I stumbled or crawled to the bathroom. Wrenched up
the music note by note. Slept so hard, I forgot how madly
I danced in a darkness that drove me. I didn't know
where I was going. Only that I wanted to get to
what is next. I wave back.
Can she see me or did she stop seeing me years before as
we ate in silence at the kitchen table?—Where
in the measured quiet I pictured my father not gone. His
head bowed. Blessing the food. His voice extended in prayer.
Me pretending meekness when I whispered my verse—
Jesus wept.
I don't cry that I carry silence with me. Have thrown it
into mis-matched suitcases and will wear it like old underwear
to all my college classes. Nobody needs to see what
has sobered me—what I carry underneath.

A TASTE

My aunt bursts through the door as if
pushed by ghost hands. She chokes a
bulging paper bag with a twisted neck.
Holds it up like a trophy. The same way
my father grips the head of a chicken
after he's wrung and snapped its neck.
The chicken's body runs without a head
the way I move sometimes, fast, without
thinking, in a chaotic rush to get beyond
the kitchen and a woman's job to cook
for rich people. I get chipped saucers as
she jokes about backdoor advantages.
Splits the bag open at the spot softened
by juice. I blurt, Shrimp. Never more than
five or six. Stuffed heavy with crabmeat,
they fall away from each other like my
father who never joins us in the kitchen.
Says he's watching a game or the news.
Eleven years from now when I graduate
from college, he will tell me that he was
not going to be controlled with table
scraps. And I will briefly feel ashamed
for having been teased into craving meaty
Kalamata olives purple-black as irises that
bloomed on the side of our house in late
spring. I will remember how green and
pink dessert mints wobbled to the edge of
the table and tumbled reluctantly into my
cupped hand. How their powdery sweet
still catches me off balance.

HARD SWEETNESS

Scratch is handed down for learning.
My mother in the kitchen. Every Sunday teaching
how to make a pound cake in the dented pan.
Oddly shaped. Uniquely beautiful. She said,

1 cup butter
chunks of careful strictness
1 cup milk
softens dry breakfast cereal
2 cups sugar
sweet kiss on my lips when
I leave for school
3 cups flour
smooth-thick rhythms sifted
through low pitch chastising
4 eggs
cracked open for my daddy's
voice to slip out of me
1½ teaspoons baking powder
to increase volume of my voice
full of sweat and fist in protest
1 teaspoon lemon flavoring
warns do not dare pucker my
lips to say one word
1 teaspoon vanilla flavoring
she said just enough to be
delicately sweet

Cream butter & sugar, add heart.
Pour mixture into pan. Bake 350°,
one hour—maybe 10, 15 minutes
extra if need more heat to rise up.

Let sit and cool 10 minutes.

Do not frost with shame.

AMERICAN BEAUTY: ALL THE RAGE DARKLY

1.
A certain amount of the feminine narcissism must rest ultimately on real physical attactiveness

The girl who is black
Her blackness is   creamy   her lips are thick, her hair is kinky and short. She, is in fact, the   thesis of American beauty.
loved and prized   by her mother, family, and community, she has   basis of feminine attractiveness on which to build a sound feminine narcissism.

2.
In an addition, she takes her place within a historical context, in which

3.
the achievement of a healthy, mature womanhood seems a   miracle

WHAT WE LEARNED

You were on the wild side, she says after
decades and, remind me, what's your name?
But I'm stuck on wild.

How could she have forgotten my name?
Imply I was animalian, raving mad, worse,
self-willed because I was the only girl,
back then, labeled Negro in an ocean of
four hundred white splashes.

When I say my name, Marge says, That's
right, like one of our high school teachers
quizzing, checking my understanding to
assure everywhere in this world

I learn my untamed place.

That I see myself as a secretary with a carved
juju face. Maybe a short-necked giraffe
chewing a cud at Starbucks, or a wild boar
screeching in city traffic or just

a domesticated something.

Like my mother, a domestic working woman,
like my two grandmothers and great grands.
I push down that old have-to-keep up feeling as
Marge announces she's a retired architect. I say
I'm a retired professor.

I still feel the uneasiness of comparison under
her upturned nostrils as if to catch a whiff
of some trait that will mark me.

Turns out we were at the same college at
the same time. Surprised, she wants to know
how I heard about this poetry reading and what
I am doing here.

As if answers, which I never get to say, don't
matter, she keeps talking fast and non-stop, like
she's on stage delivering a monologue. Tidbits
about her hip replacement are a perfect segue to
make her appear to have been worked to the bone.

She raves of how she deserves to sleep in. Have
time for a morning latte—off to Tai-chi in the park
and ta-ta, her two hands flit and I don't hear
another word she says.

I'm thinking about the lessons each of us were
taught in school. Remembering how young
we were together, learning

our separate lives.

4.

HARD SWEETNESS

Scratch is my mother's raw-sweet.

Said some of us would have to die.

Said some trees still wear clothes

ATROPA BELLADONNA

I wanted to tell you Dad, but never did. That first night you slept at home after
years in the state hospital for the criminally insane, I was scared to death. When

I walked into the dark of your room just past one, I didn't know then that began
the hour guards did their checking. I only wanted socks from the dresser drawer.

Sliding scrunch of wood rubbing wood must have awakened how those guards
tore into you. Your flesh taut under pressure of grunt. What in hell are you doing,

is what you shouted. The fight in your voice dug into me. Unearthed my buried
silence. Like a stalk, my body tensed in the uprooting. I unraveled. Uncontrollable,

under the sound of fear, my stomach shook like clumps and crumbled. I thought
you were going to kill me. Kill me dead, Dad. I had heard what doctors who claimed

to be real doctors said. Joked that you were schizoid-frantic. Will snap at any moment.
And, I thought, This is the moment those doctors talked about. I bolted. Ran barefoot—

wild and slipped on dew-swollen grass in the carbon-black night. The air, delightfully
pungent, made me woozy in darkness—my constant remedy. I'm glad you did not

chase after me. I would have screamed, punched up at you with all the beauty of a
belladonna bursting with murderous berries, my fists swinging ferociously, until
I crumpled, one knee down—half-praying
to hug you.

FINDINGS FORM A PATTERN

Said Uncle C.
𝓕 doesn't belong there.
They will keep on him until he does
something that will give them reason
to keep him (where men have died
during or after beatings by guards.)

Said Old Man D.
Common sense will
tell you that 𝓕 didn't belong there
At that time being black was way worse
(where men have been pummeled
senseless for sport.)

Said Woman E.
𝓕 was clear as he always was (where
there is no treatment aside from mood-
altering drugs). If they damaged him it
didn't show. 𝓕 was still a nice guy.

Said Neighbor Boy C.
We all wished 𝓕 was our dad. Stood up
like a man. Didn't back down. Made his
own way.

Said people who share the darkest black.

OAK SIDE BBQ

For half a dozen/six-in-one-hand
years, a man is packed. Warehoused.
Stored like frozen meat. Not for sale
from the butcher's block this time.

For half a dozen/six-in-one-hand
summers after that, lucky-to-be-alive
limbs thaw on the tree side of a house.
Baby back ribs sizzle on the backyard grill.
Charred meat burns tenderly pungent as
a corpse flower blooming.

The man slops the bones with homemade
sauce. His wife slices a watermelon with
a butcher-knife. Examines the rind for
degree of ripeness. Sees how the juicy red
seeps to brown a stem hardened to
sweetness.

Glossy seed-eyes see memory of blossoms
and roots. See the man's reconfigured body.
Not strange fruit hanging, but the trunk
standing thick skinned. Two feet planted in
soil. Clutching new green.

FIGURES

1. Figuration
   Post Card. Correspondence.
   Scrawled in brown ink. A son
   writes on the back.
   Dear Mother,

   This is the
   Barbecue we
   had last Night
   My picture is to
   the left With a
   cross over it Your
   son, Joe.

FIGURES

2. Configuration.
   Signifying atonement.
   Homage to the man not seen.
   His body hanging as an object being
   erased. See the cross among the disciples
   now? An ink smudge above Joe's head
   like a crown handed down to a believer.
   To carry on the teaching.

TRINKET

…before June, 1965, when a chauffeur is disappeared…gone–dead

Get your wife a little something the rich lady
said at a rest-stop along the Pennsylvania turnpike,
when my father chauffeured her all the way to
the nation's capital.

He picked out a porcelain boxer dog. Umber
brown with two pups, and the rich lady paid.
Each pup was connected with a metal loop
that held a small chain linked to the mother's
collared neck.

What is left of that vintage set is one crippled
pup with three whole legs and a hind one gone
up to the tibia.

Though the break is smooth and shows creamy
porcelain flesh beneath, the appearance of
rawness reminds me that the body holds hurt.
How it keeps absence like an open wound that
never heals.

After wiping its dusty coat, it shines as if my
father had just brought it home brand new to
my mother who loved trinkets. Puppyish in her
love for small things, she placed the three dogs
on the homemade shelf mounted on the wall.
A gift to be awed, out of reach and beyond what
we could afford.

Looking at the pup doesn't make me feel sorry.
I keep it because it charms like a coveted heirloom.
It is what is left of the giving. A lineage that even
in its deformity stands as what need not be spoken.

Although the hind leg is a stump, placed a certain way, the pup can stand on three legs. It looks as if if it might buckle, but the body makes do. What's missing is not missed. It is a way to understand that torn away is not dead but life rearranged.

HOW A BODY

The pup's body is like my father's. Home after
years in the gone-dead place where guards' boots
crushed his shin bone. Home to morning coffee,
toast and one scrambled egg, his leg drags across
the kitchen floor and reminds how a body redistributes
weight of loss. How a body dares to keep standing.

HIS VOICE ON BRANCHES

Out back, I find my father in a lawn chair.
Its aluminum legs misshaped like the awkward
ache I feel as I walk toward him. Frayed green
and white strips of plastic are crisscrossed like
potholders I made in seventh grade. It is the way
we are. My mind struggles to twist loose ends
together. To put time in order. Time before. Time
during. Time now: to learn my father after a long
separation is a lesson in roaming the woods.
There is no name I can give being unsettled. It
is like, and not like, what I felt seeing Uncle Fred
in a casket at the old Baptist church. I leaned in
and put my lips on his. Until then I had never
kissed a dead man. I wanted to make it mean
something but didn't know what. I don't know
what it means now when I call through a muddle
of color. Say, Dad. He's swearing into the new
green woods as if words will snag on branches of
a plum tree. Blossom and bear luscious fruits
with pits hidden by dense foliage. I stand mute as
pebbles scattered creek-side. Stiff, in the slow
measured twist of his neck as he turns carefully
within his reliable brown skin. Steadily, bringing
his body back, he keeps coming home like waking.
Blinking two, three, a hundred times and shaking
his head clear. His eyes are streaked as a cardinal
zipping past petals of forsythia. The cautious red.
Anxious yellow. I bend. Kiss the bald spot on his
head. Hold my lips there.

WHAT SOIL MAKES

Out of the gone-dead sanctuary a man
emerges with a dream of free. Beneath
flesh and inside his bones is marrow of
future. Though his bare shoulders curl
inward, I ache to see the muscular bulk
of his back bent under the hood of his
red pick-up. The one he painted his name
on, free-hand, to show ownership. He
added…and Sons, hoping to pass on,
not a landscaping business, but ability to
belong to oneself. My brothers laughed
when they saw it, each falling into
the other. Their boy bodies soft as
summer soil as they hugged in their frailty.
I did not laugh. I could see what my
father's eyes held. Though, I am not a boy,
I picked up a rake and dragged its rusted
teeth across patches of wilted grass. In
each small ditch of earth, I dropped seeds,
covered them with dirt and kneeled to offer
handfuls of water to grow a new start. My
brothers could never dream as free as my
father. To re-seed. Begin again in the soil
of flesh and endure tenderness of new
growth. Cut and shape twigs of forsythia
to prepare for bursts of yellow blossoms.
Dig up half-wit stumps. Plant two yews
with roots that grow straight through eyes
of the dead. Hold them tethered down
under. My brothers can never be green
again. No ambition to unload dumps of
steaming manure. Shovel shit, never, they
said,…will not plant geraniums and
peonies, ever. And, one small detail about
the phone number painted on the truck—
they knew it by heart.

MY MOTHER'S HAIR

It is over. I stroke my mother's hair.
Her head is in my lap. Her body is stretched out
on the couch. Mine is pressed into its arm.
A man's dying has exhausted my expectation.
He wrote on a scrap of paper, Where's…, before
letters became scribble, he became unconscious,
and I don't know what is where.

I stroke my mother's hair,

feel her fatigue supple on my thighs as she curls,
gives her head completely to my strength. Both
knees are like knots on branches of the front-yard
maple. The clavicle sculpted so exquisitely, I see
what has been carved from years of love shaped
with care.

 I don't dare touch it.

I'm afraid the bone will ping. That I will hear again
how that day began. The doctor shut the door.
Left us cramped in a family room around a table,
natural as eating dinner in our small kitchen where
brothers' faces begged no more mashed potatoes,
though they love the way she makes them.
Sister's eyes dropped.

I heard the stalling

in my mother's voice. To pull the plug or not. She
asked me. No. She forced me. No. She trusted me
to come to the right conclusion. And, I knew what
I had to say.

BIRD WATCH DECEMBER, 1992

My father teaches me again to sit quietly and
still, as if in the silence I heard him say, Listen.
Don't butt into grown folk's business, and go
sit down. And I would, but not for long. When
my brother spots a huge bird, unidentifiable,
wobbling for balance over Route 910, he blurts,
Look, with such force of surprise, I can't help
screaming, I see it. Wings too heavy for its speck
of body. Between paddling, dipping, then lifting
I see a tail like a tiny baby's butt. The skin bald
and innocent. My brother says the bird doesn't
look like it belongs in Pennsylvania. I ask,
What bird does?

I imagine my father is the bird that cracked open
the shell of a man nearly worn to dust. What's
left lay in a copper colored casket in the hearse up
ahead. That car is far darker than the cobalt blue
one he drove as a chauffeur. Chest out. Cap straight.
Now he rides the backseat situated and untethered
in his tan pinstriped suit he put on for dress-up
occasions. Like the time my brother got married in
a Jehovah Witness preacher's dimly lit apartment.
Then the time he put it on for his sister's funeral but
didn't go—sat on the porch and smoked cigarette
after cigarette. When it was new he wore it to
a family reunion and spilled a glass of wine on
the cuff of a sleeve. The red seeped in and faded but
left a mark.

Leaving this world the bird breaks waves of clouds.
Drops to a lower altitude. I pay attention to keep it
in sight, watch it without saying a word. In my head
I assure myself, it's guiding me to the place between
two oak trees my father told me about. The plot of
land my mother said she didn't want to hear where
it was. That she didn't want to think of that place
anywhere on Earth.

BETTER THAN WHITNEY HOUSTON

She was at the sink wringing a dish cloth. Then
wiping the aluminum cabinets above in long
sweeps and stretching up on tippy-toes as her
voice reached higher and a long breath rested on
the *I*, before she brought the cloth to water and
started the chorus again. And I sat there quiet as
a mouse like she used to say when thunder rolled
in. She never turned to look at me, but I heard
what the thunder said. She kept her arm swaying
steady left to right as if it were a metronome
keeping time until her voice became a whisper as
if into my father's ear a far-reaching promise of
will always.

The kitchen was at quiet attention too. No fork
scratching against a chipped plate. No refrigerator
humming to keep tempo. Clicking hands of
the wall clock stuck in stutter as if to hold time
for a brief moment to gather emotions in a world
struck by lightning. When the second hand lurched
forward it ignited the muscle that sings to survive.
It began to coo *love you* so sweetly the sound lifted
like a new bird taking its first flight into the storm.
And I sat there, so quiet.

5.

HARD SWEETNESS

My mother killed my sweet eyes.

She said, *See.*

A SMALL SUICIDE

Again and again the house-finch barrels its body headfirst
into the living room window. Keeps up its frantic flight until
the fourth plunk sends the small thing crashing to the porch.

It is either unconscious or dead. I watch it before getting on
with culling the snap peas. Look intently to detect a slight
flutter of a feather. Nothing. I leave it.

After an hour I check. There it lay, still as a fence post. I
wonder how long it takes for a bird to die from crashing into
its own reflection—attracted to the hunger it sees inside itself
that makes it want to get at that faceless dark body.

When I peer again I feel a twitch of empathy growing inside
the space in which I see myself. I can spare a bit for a kindred
life trying hard to get to the inside. To fly into spaces where
darkness is shaped by light and displayed as a shadow.

The little finch lay quiet and unknowable, reminding me how
silent hurt can be, how it can lay stiff in fragile bones. All night
I dream of the bird. How cute it is, if it will be there in
the morning. Will it have come to its senses and flown away into
the madness of branches?

Or, will a hungry predator—an owl, a nighthawk, or a prowling
cat—find delicious the small mouthful of desperation with which
the bird struggled to be at one with itself before falling together
with its own image.

I have been warned that death seeks the darkness in you.

AMERICAN BEAUTY: THE REDRESS

That cube shaped four room structure on Lincoln Drive,
the black dirt road that curves, not without the bend

of backs of men and women, calloused hands softened
by the steady shine of stars, flakes of carbon bodies
perfectly aligned in black space, could be called glimmers,

by another name, children. And, when I grew up to be a
teacher, my parents were happy the way relentless rays
bear down on the body, permeate,

fuse with a deeper dust beyond the boney dump of cinders
and ashes. I wish you could have seen their faces, how
the violet's slender stem offered up

its purple petal flora, emanated an aura and further back in
the woods, fauna, and time before I taught, I was announced
township queen. An aluminum tiara was fixed on my head.

Plastic crystals dangled light prismed in transparent hardness.
At the right angle, I saw rainbows. From another angle,
streaks of light did not arc into colors. White ones said

Black Beauty. No compliment. Anger has its pinch. On
the front yard trellis, what red, red rose doesn't appreciate
thorns spiking its stem?—prickly and curl-tipped. Protectors

that guarantee survival of the wiles of humans and other
animals. So, you can imagine the other contestants' ire when
their intent was exposed, how weedy they appeared when

asked, What is the most important thing our society needs?—
and each girl bared more teeth than the one before she replied
with something that seemed smart and caring, like World Peace.

GIRL, DIVINE

Two miles down in the dark, I turn left onto
a dirt road that leads to Bob-Ray's junk yard.
Squeeze through a barbed wire fence where
I have trampled bramble and burr training
my body to weave between thickets and not
get scratched deep enough to bleed. I sneak
past piles of scrap iron and salvageable pieces
of machinery that can be screwed or welded to
make something broken whole again. Like
a body closed off after being wrecked.

The old mare I've come for is tied with a rope to
a banged-up car door. It stirs and dances a rusty
trot until it recognizes my scent. It's like times
I've walked up on those who knew me well but
still got the jitters. That's how I learned the nature
of an animal to be a beast. I pet the long neck.
Untie the rope. Lead it into the night and ride
bareback to the road behind my house. Race up
and down to see its hide turn silvery-brown in
skeins of moonlight.

I let the rope fly. No need to hold back. Blackness
has its own charge. I hug the thick neck and feel
matted mane against my cheek as I lean into altitudes
of freedom. With legs pressed against side barrel
muscles, I dig my heels in until I feel passion rage in
my pores. Wild as Pegasus must have felt bursting
from Medusa's neck drenched in the capacity
to be divine.

ONE INFINITE MOMENT AT THE MAJESTIC TRUCK STOP

Staring from behind the counter a teenage girl
looks bewildered and innocent. She can't take her eyes
off me.

I know these moments of silence. I stare back and only
because there are people behind me I blurt, Coffee. She
doesn't ask small, medium or large.

She doesn't move. I don't either.

I'm remembering the way time seemed dream-like in
seventh grade right before a rich girl kicked my shin with
her cordovan loafer. Screamed, nigger.

I want to scream now, Don't you see me standing right here,
waiting for you to be of service?

From behind her ketchup-stained white apron. From
behind the white shirt with a fly-away collar and a white
disposable paper hat bobby-pinned to her hair, she
keeps looking. —still doesn't say a word.

I say, Black

and keep looking straight into glass-green eyes that
show befuddlement and—does the squinching nose mean
she's questioning the everyday pinch of hot exhaust,
funk of sweaty flesh and caustic smell of fried onions?

Or, is the question hanging in the air between us?—
irreconcilable as our bodies... Each on our own side of
the counter.

Not budging. Like I stood before I went blind in a
millisecond and my fists raged when the rich girl's loafer
struck mid-bone. And don't I remember a shiny copper Lincoln
gleaming from inside the lip-like strap cut across the vamp?

What is this teen-girl saying without sound—is she dumbstruck
or is she dumb?

I say, The coffee… Black.

She gets it.

CANCELLED ORDER

1.
A flagrant finger points. Takes aim.
I'm glad it isn't a pistol. The waitress
would have pulled the trigger. I would
have slumped over. My head knocking
against the sticky café table. And, I
would not have heard the poet reading
her poem. I would not have had to say
three times that I am cancelling my order.
The waitress would not have had to
demand, You have to pay, for the first time,
or a second. Or, the third time before she
slammed a plate of hot wingdings in front
of me. One wing would not have rolled
from the plate and I would not have sensed
a meat avalanche. Her body hovering.
Leaning in to smother me under the cold
tumble of her voice insisting that I stop
breathing.

2.
If I do as she presses—in the obit section
of the local gazette my name will appear as
a bold bleed of black ink. My first name
misspelled with the i before the e. And, it
will go on to say I was a local poet survived
by other local poets. That I was not following
unstated and unwritten policies. That my
composure agitated the waitress and I dared
mince words with a calm that resisted. The
waitress will be called a victim. I will be
named the aggressor.

3.

Two sentences later, words will say murder
was justified. The waitress who gave birth two
months before, and to be fair, had baby blues
which gave her the right to take my breath. It
will not say she leaned in too far. That she was
angry about who was to serve whom.

MAKING NICE

I throw the walker she named Harry into the trunk of my car. As I drive over
smooth pavement, past Tudor style homes and sidewalks lined with trees,
Bobbie's voice is in my ear.

She complains about her Uncle Ralph from Cali, as if I know him personally.
Or want to. She says he can't stand our new President—says, that Kenyan will
ruin him. That she's not like him and some of her best friends are…

Why does Bobbie want to make nice?
To make me feel more…what?
To make herself look more…what?
What is the what?

My body begins its transformation. Herecomesthisshitagain unraveling and
slidingthroughmygut. I'm holding my Promethean fire. Without taking a breath,
she says the man won't give her a dime. Mocks his voice as she offers one of
his favorite jokes. Goes like this she says,

Did you hear the one
about how many…
it takes to lynch a…?

I feel Prometheus bringing fire. I'm seething. Why does Bobbie think I need
to know what her Uncle Ralph thinks is funny? To make nice? To make herself
appear to have fallen farther from the tree?

My foot pushes the gas pedal. She keeps bearing down on rich Uncle Ralph. He's
got more money than you can imagine. Her face pinks up as I watch her hand
point five curled arthritic fingers in five directions until she yells, Make a right.
Here. A right. Right. Here.

She keeps talking into the quick turn, through the lean of her body about how she
can't stand Uncle Ralph's ways—especially when he says, I hate that Kenyan.

I'm leaning, too and say, Are you sure he says Kenyan?

She half turns her head to stare out of the passenger window at lush green lawns with houses set back on a storybook street. In slow motion her lips twist up. She talks to grass and brick—says, Yeah. Kenyan.

OFF EXIT 99

Straight ahead is a John Deere Equipment Company. Pristine green
and yellow tractors and trucks look like toys. Instinctively, I lower
my music before I turn left onto a dirt road toward a small town called
New Castle. The stretch of full green extends my imagination. Trees
bend along the roadside. Maybe they were planted for shade. Maybe
they were planted to hover or to hide. They are hauntingly beautiful.
Farther down on the right is a tall marquee. Black letters raised on
dusty white plastic make me think the sign lights up to a dim yellow
at night. Getting closer I read, *Grace's Monuments Sold Her*. I think
the final 'e' must be missing. But maybe it isn't missing. It makes
sense even with the letter not there. It still could be a certain kind of
advertisement or message. I creep cautiously until I see bodies locked
behind a tall, link fence. None move. The field is full of them. All
made to lean in a stiff pose of servitude. All their faces are Mars-black
in yellow-ochre sunlight. Each cast-iron hand holds a lantern ready to
illuminate the coming dark.

SIDEWALK SUICIDE (ATTEMPT)

My neighbor sits in a lawn chair he's carried
from his porch to the sidewalk. I have already
seen him see me and look away. I make myself
visible despite how he wants to not see me. I say,
Hey Mike, how are you doing, but I'm thinking,
This man is deranged. His body is naked from
the waist up. His back, a pale tawny-pink. He
doesn't say he's fine or even okay. He says he's
trying to have a stroke. His face is red. His hair
is chaotic as if he has been running his fingers
through it trying to organize his thoughts. It sticks
out like spikey proteins on a ball of corona virus.
His face is desperately tragic. I think he really
wants to die. And, for a miniscule of time, I admit,
I want him to drop right then. It is a moment of
accumulated stares tearing at my body. I clench
my teeth to hold back impulse. The rush of rage
for insulting compliments given generously. How
he wishes he was in my eighth grade class as if
I would hug him close and remind him of his
beautiful potential. But that is beyond this moment.
Beyond what I think is right or just. Raw urge
makes me feel like conquering. In a surge of
fiery magma I lock my eyes with his and in my
most searing voice, I spit like a curse, You have
to learn how to live like the rest of us.

PRICK AT THE PHYSICAL THERAPY REHAB CLINIC

5 a.m. and she is sticking a needle in my right arm hanging
over the side of the bed. She is taking blood enough to
fill three tiny test tubes. Make sure I don't get a clot after
hip surgery.

It can happen. And you can die, a lady behind me said at
the grocery store five days ago.

I don't know if the prick woke me or if it was the slap to get
the vein up in the crook of my elbow. The thick rubber-band
tourniquet feels tighter than what is needed to get the vein
to bulge.

My skin is a twisted pinch. I think she did it on purpose. I'm
unearthly groggy but I can still feel.

Fell asleep the night before, when the count was turning toward
disaster. But I was hopeful. The oxycodone was great for making
beautiful images come to mind and I should have written
them down.

Not to worry I told myself. I'll remember the pantsuit. Her royal
purple one foretelling a regal victory for sure.

The nurse is hunched over my arm which she has pulled in and
pinned to her body. I know not to move and mess everything up.
She would have to slap and prick again. Her hair is sticking up
like a straw broom.

Her black roots are showing. Her breath is a husky wheeze and is
condensing on my skin.

I start to move my mouth. My jaw muscles are heavy and stiff. It takes a long time to get words out but I manage to garble, Who's the President? She says one word with prick and puncture and with gusto of triumph.

I feel I have to protect myself in my vulnerability. The name almost makes me jerk my arm away.

But she has me and is pushing the needle deeper as if to say, I dare you to say one word about my President. I close my eyes. Too groggy to think clearly. Hold my breath. Hold my tongue.

i.e.

The story began before the story I'm telling
of a man teaching what he realized while he
was held in a space called gone-dead. He was
not being held in a holding pen as during
the blackest-darkness. But it is the same black.
He is telling his son this before-story because
the son will grow up to be a man who will need
to have eyes-that-see-in-the-dark.

Eyes-that-see-in-the-dark doesn't mean there is
no light. It means the man tells his son how to
read the before-story in a language with words
that illuminate. Do's and don'ts with hands and
feet, mouth and tongue. To remember, there's no
death like your Mamma loving you to death.

FIGURES

3. Dear Black Mothers,
   Reconfigured Angels
   bearing that cross and
   still wearing earrings.
   Teardrop rhinestones
   Silver hearts. Rare ebony
   rounds and circles of
   gold. Lord could have
   saved...

   This world from the mob to the river.
   Child.

   This world from a vigilante standing his ground.
   Child.

   This world with *hands up, don't shoot.*
   Child.

   This world with a toy gun.
   Child.

   And child and child and
   worlds.

   And worlds of Man.

   This one in a hail of 41 bullets.
   Man.

   This one in a chokehold.
   Man.

   This one jogging in his neighborhood.
   Man.

This one with a knee on his neck.
Man.

Man.
Child.

Man-child can't breathe in a land of promise.

etc.

The man tells his son, eyes-that-see-in-the-dark
means there is a bit of possible hope that filters
into a place where everything black is strained
through a system of penetrating light. A planned
madness that is not chaos. It is the gone-dead
place—space between the living and the dead.
Where the body walks in circles, is beaten, and
cursed. Shamed and deprived until it is taken.
Shaped into the smallest particle of flesh that has
no meaning. But alive. With breath. Barely. Not
like the shape of a boy's small hand playing with
a toy gun. Or, a grown man's lungs caved under
grip of chokehold. Not like a teen's back targeted
in hard sheen of moonlight. A neck pressed under
weight of a bent knee. Not like a young spine
severed. Or, a chest budding its heart. The story
keeps blooming. Sure to bear more fruit—i.e.
the end keeps flourishing with occasions of
sweetness. Etc., etc.

BOY AS OCCASION OF SWEETNESS

Other teachers think he is strange. It isn't
his almond colored skin. It is his eyes.
They are blue as if the ocean is in him and
the water has risen up past his lids into his
pupils. His eyes are placid. The calmness
makes teachers question. They want to know
how this ocean happened. It is odd. Makes
them uncomfortable. Doesn't make sense.
He isn't what they expect. Not mean. Not
loud. Or, a smart aleck. It would be easier
to label him a troublemaker if he had regular
eyes. It would remove him from their
discomfort. They would feel less threatened
by the way his body in motion appears to be
still. He is just a boy with a soft voice. When
he makes comments or answers questions in
class his eyes are words and his voice is held
back by a blush. When his mouth swells into
a smile his cheeks puff up as if to make his
eyes two, distant, blue suns rising together
and scattering light. Other teachers ask over
and over if I can believe such a thing as a
brown boy with blue eyes. I say, Yes, I see
him. I see how he dreams in his Air Jordans.
How his voice carries him up before his body
is a bubble bursting. Before other teachers
insist, he will never be anything. I wish they
could have seen him beyond their horizons.
How he wouldn't become a negative statistic
but graduate as a promise with a scholarship.
How he would become an engineer, featured
as an outstanding employee. See his wife, a
scientist, and their baby born with a smile.
See how he works fulltime, has his own side
business clearing weeds and making way for

planting seeds. And, the young boys he hires
are quiet. They blush, too.

6.

MEAT ON MY SOUL

1.
I am my father's tongue.
One pink variation from being
beaten with a beautifully shaped club.
A solid hickory of hate petrified
stony hard to stifle words that leap
from the mouth and dive beneath the skin.

I say, *Touch here*, where two
lie bumps pulse, white-tipped as
a red-hot poker that burns silence into
the skin. Marked by men who

pulled my father from his pick-up and
beat him due to variation on the meaning
of voice from one hundred to one-sixteenth
percent echo found in the blood.

The lie bumps shoot pain even when
the sweetest tastes roll over them. How
those cops must have loved the scroll of my
father's blood. The bedtime story their knuckles
told to teach their children to savor this
standard deviation of aftertaste.

Even before I learned the lies, my father
licked his own lesions to heal me. Five grains of
salt placed on the tip of his index finger until
granules huddled inside the spittle, formed a
pasty asafetida pressed against utterances
geneticized with intent to deviate from True North—
a slight etymologic derivation of how
free speech means, *Pull here*, where the rope
is slack, and a mute tongue
will slip sideways.

2.

I am my father's articulate female-tongue which
cannot be unlearned. I am the thick-thigh voice of
omission, the fatback talk of three-fifths torso,
one-eighth red black blood and a straight-up
mouthful of words that are straight-up-uppity.
Troublesome to some.

I don't humble down, play shut-mouthed or lay low
my tongue until I have out-dogged the dogs and
the hounds have quieted their barking.

Here. Right here. At the tip of my tongue, I nurse
two white festering bumps full of lies that burn like
hell. For a few days the small inflammations will be
tender—truth is—my father's salty finger-tip on
my tongue is ceremony, a burning of memory into
my flesh.

See here, me, a tree-woman with a rooted trunk and
strong branches—arms full of abundant blossoms.
I say, *Look right here at this* and point to the two
scars on my tongue where my father's love healed.

Marked me as a variation of sweetness.

NOTES

Poems in sections 1 and 2 chart personal and historical incidents of the time my father was held in a state hospital for the criminally insane during the 1960's fight for Civil Rights. Some of the details were pulled from newspaper articles in *The Philadelphia Inquirer*, written by journalists Acel Moore and Wendell Rawls, Jr. in 1976. The book *Cold Storage* (Simon and Schuster, 1980) by Wendell Rawls, Jr., and a broadcast found in The Studs Terkel's Radio Archive titled, "Wendell Rawls, Jr. discusses his book 'Cold Storage'" (Broadcast Date: Feb. 29, 1980) provided additional research information. I also had personal meetings and phone conversations with both Acel Moore and Wendell Rawls, Jr.

"His Body Holds Silence": *Zong* is the name of a slave ship where the massacre of 130 sick Africans took place at the hands of British slavers. On November 29th 1781, these Africans were thrown overboard so the British slavers could claim a loss of property with their insurers and receive payment.

"American Beauty: 101" and "American Beauty: All The Rage Darkly" are poems from the book *Black Rage* (Basic Books, Inc., 1993) by William H. Grier and Price M. Cobbs.

"Meat on My Soul": *Lie bumps* are painful little white or red bumps on the tongue like taste buds that have become enlarged, irritated, swollen, or split. The word comes from an old wives' tale that blamed the bumps for telling lies.

NOTES ON THE PHOTOGRAPHS

Page 20: An old photo of my father as a boy around age four.

Page 40: The poem titled "Small Hands" is a photo of me at around age two.

Page 86: The photograph in the poem "Figures" (which has been graphically distorted) is the front side of a postcard which can be found in the book *Without Sanctuary* (Twin Palms Publishers, 2000) by James Allen.

Page 89: A photo of the boxer pup referred to in the poems "Trinket" and "How A Body."

Page 102: A newspaper photo of me seated front and center, wearing the Miss Indiana Township tiara and banner, with a bouquet of flowers in the poem titled "The Tiara."

ACKNOWLEDGMENTS

Thank you to the editors of the publications where the following poems or some versions of the poems have appeared:

Anthology of Appalachian Writers, Volume XIV: "Keeping Track," "A Taste";
Pittsburgh Poetry Review: "Used Slippers";
Pittsburgh Post-Gazette: "What We Learned";
South Dakota Review, V. 56, No. 4: "What Soil Makes," "Girl Divine," "Used
    Slippers";
Voices from the Attic: "No Fudging";
Vox Populi: "What We Learned."

I am grateful Richard Blanco for your careful attention to this body of work, without such brilliance and patience this book would not have come into existence. Thank you to Carlow University's MFA Program in which many of these poems were birthed and to Tess Barry, its director, for always reminding me that I am a poet. Thank you Toi Derricott and Cornelius Eady for founding Cave Canem which provided a safe space for my voice. And thank you Cave Canem family for your constant encouragement whenever and wherever we meet. Thank you Lee Ann Roripaugh for your expert eyes and insights. Thank you Jaki Shelton Green for your steadfastness in sharing with me the value of African American history as documented in poetry. Thank you Acel Moore and Wendall Rawls, Jr. for leading me to the pertinent information needed to bring light to many of the poems. Thank you Andy Muñoz for the suggestion to include images that leave a lasting impression. Thank you Carolyn Matthews, Celeste Gainey, and Bonita Penn for proofing my initial manuscript. Thank you Sue Holme for typing and formatting the manuscript. Thank you Aracelis Girmay, without whom this collection would not have found a home.

Thank you to my siblings and especially to my husband, Bruce, who dared to continue to lend an ear to every single poem. Thank you Stella and Debbie Martinez for summer evenings on your porch gazing at the mountains as the sun set over Taos and I could take a much needed rest.

Every Hard Sweetness is a debt of gratitude I offer to my parents, Marcia and Frank Carter, who gave everything to carefully raise a black girl to carry on as their living dream. Thank you mom and dad.

ABOUT THE AUTHOR

Sheila L. Carter-Jones taught in the Pittsburgh Public Schools and in Chatham University's and the University of Pittsburgh's Education Departments. She earned her BA from Carnegie Mellon University and both a M.Ed. and Ph.D. from the University of Pittsburgh. Sheila also holds a National Board of Professional Teaching Standard Certification in Early Adolescence English Language Arts and a North American Montessori Certification. Sheila is a fellow of the Western Pennsylvania Writer's Project as well as a fellow of both the Pittsburgh Teachers Institute and the Yale National Initiative.

Sheila's manuscript *Three Birds Deep* was selected by Elizabeth Alexander as the 2012 winner of the Naomi Long Madgett Poetry Book Award and her chapbook *Crooked Star Dream Book* was named runner-up for the 2013 New York Center for Book Arts Chapbook Contest. Sheila is a fellow of Cave Canem, the home for African American poets and other poets of color. She is also a fellow of the Callaloo Creative Writing Workshop and a Walter Dakins Fellow of the 2015 Sewanee Writer's Conference. Her poetry has been published in several journals, anthologies, and magazines. She is the Co-founder of (sub)Verses Social Collective, a platform for the voices of African American women and women of color in the community. Sheila earned her MFA from Carlow University.

BOA EDITIONS, LTD. AMERICAN POETS CONTINUUM SERIES

No. 199 *Buffalo Girl*
        Jessica Q. Stark
No. 200 *Nomenclatures of Invisibility*
        Mahtem Shiferraw
No. 201 *Flare, Corona*
        Jeannine Hall Gailey
No. 202 *Death Prefers the Minor Keys*
        Sean Thomas Dougherty
No. 203 *Desire Museum*
        Danielle Deulen
No. 204 *Transitory*
        Subhaga Crystal Bacon
No. 205 *Every Hard Sweetness*
        Sheila Carter-Jones

COLOPHON

BOA Editions, Ltd., a not-for-profit publisher of poetry
and other literary works, fosters readership and appreciation
of contemporary literature. By identifying, cultivating, and publishing both new
and established poets and selecting authors of unique literary talent, BOA brings
high-quality literature to the public.

Support for this effort comes from the sale of its publications, grant funding, and
private donations.

~

*The publication of this book is made possible, in part,
by the special support of the following individuals:*

Anonymous (x2)

Blue Flower Arts, LLC

Angela Bonazinga & Catherine Lewis

Daniel R. Cawley

David J. Fraher

Andrew & Karen Gallina

Margaret B. Heminway

Nora A. Jones

Paul LaFerriere & Dorrie Parini, *in honor of Bill Waddell*

Barbara Lovenheim

Joe McElveney

John H. Schultz

William Waddell & Linda Rubel